Poetry NonScenes

Poetry Non-Scenes

New performance poems beyond the struggle

Compiled and introduced by Tom Penfold, Adam Levin and Deirdre Byrne

uHlanga
2024

Poetry NonScenes
POETRYNONSCENES.COM

Introduction © the editors, 2024, all rights reserved
Selection of poems © the editors, 2024, all rights reserved
Individual poems © the named authors, 2024, all rights reserved

First published in Durban, South Africa by uHlanga in 2024
UHLANGAPRESS.CO.ZA

This edition is distributed print-on-demand by African Books Collective

ISBN: 978-1-0370-1148-1

Edited by Tom Penfold, Adam Levin and Deirdre Byrne
Cover design and typesetting by Nick Mulgrew
Proofread by Jennifer Jacobs

This book is set in Wavehaus Sans

The opinions and views expressed in this volume are not necessarily those held by its publisher or any associated institution.

THIS ANTHOLOGY IS A PROJECT OF

WITH THE SUPPORT OF

Introduction 9

Part I: Conflict

Mirrors	**Shade K. Olugbosi** 14
The Only Thing Left	**Dshamilja Roshani** 16
Time Echoes of Sorrow	**Amanda Majola** 21
Genocide	**Elizabeth Makanha-Dhliwayo** 22
The Water in Gaza	**Kiara Braum** 23
Maja	**Denise Newfield** 25

Part II: Bodies and Emotions

Children in their Twenties	**Rachel Freeme** 28
Languishing on my Bed	**Katlego Malema** 29
Wall Street	**Ivai Nyamutsamba** 30
The Collector	**Sharon Rose** 32
October 23	**Tshegofatso Masemola** 34
The God of Bonsai	**Nicole Best** 35
Border Gate	**Katlego Choshi** 36
Depression	**Delyne Nyasha Madziva** 37
This is a Poem	**Kekana Phologo** 39
Baby	**Busisiwe Kgosi** 40
Ink	**Sabrina Alho** 41

Part III: **Gender and Identity**

Dear Black Boys
Making Tea
The Epic Quest for Socks
Armed with a Smile
African
How is My Hair?
... Flashes!
Springbok
I Miss the Dolls And Toys
The Portrait of a
   South Asian Woman
The Burnt Pot
I Am

Ntokozo Twala 44
Ilanit Furman 47
Tania Nobantu Ngindana 48
Jolene Raison 49
Sandisiwe Dlamini 51
Olive Olusegun 52
Mpho Mametja 55
Imange Lobese 58
Choaro Letsoha 59

Diyoni Harisinghe 60
Leya Muthen 61
Laeeqa Ebrahim 62

About the editors 66

Introduction

There have always been crucial performative aspects to poetry in South Africa. Moreover, it has proved a genre tightly wedded to the political moment and the various battles for social and political liberation that have defined the country over the last century. One of its prominent themes is that of struggle. This remains true in the present. In the wake of the 2012 Marikana Massacre, and the 2015-16 #RhodesMustFall and #FeesMustFall student protests a new decolonial ethos emerged in South Africa's petulant democracy. This took into account the dynamics of sexuality and gender, as well as racial liberation. Amidst these turbulent changes, poetry once again experimented, performed, challenged and defined the moment.

Yet, despite poetry's evolving omnipresence in the social and political scene, poetry within the academic space has largely remained confined to yesteryear's tight understandings of 'struggle'. It also tends to be monolingual and misses the dynamic nature of the present moment in which performance takes place. The highly contested antagonism between poets of the page and poets of the stage continues to entrench Westernised notions of what counts as literature. It is our intention in this anthology to break down such barriers and to open the literary space to all, regardless of the forms of expression they wish to use.

All the contributions in the following pages result from two workshops held in April 2024 under the Poetry NonScenes banner. This project, funded by University College London, seeks to promote performance poetry, especially but not exclusively amongst the youth, and in turn challenge the largely sterile academic view of poetry described above. The poems that emerged from these events are crafted by a very diverse mixture of school learners, university students, and working professionals from South Africa's Gauteng region. The participants included learners from a wide range of Johannesburg schools (former Model C schools, private schools, and township schools).

The workshops were run in partnership with the South African Poetry Project (ZAPP), a collective of professional poets, academic researchers, and teachers who are dedicated to promoting the teaching, writing, and research of contemporary South African poetry within South African schools and local communities. Together with award-winning slam poet and Poetry Zone ZA founder Mandisa Vundla, ZAPP members facilitated the workshops, and hosted a showcase which offered an opportunity for the participants to perform their poetry to a live audience.

The first workshop was held at the Johannesburg Holocaust and Genocide Centre and many of the contributions within these pages respond directly to the Centre's permanent exhibition which brings the Holocaust into dialogue with the 1994 genocide in Rwanda. The second workshop, held at the University of Pretoria, loosely centred on the theme of emotion as poets sought to push beyond South Africa's political 'struggle'. Placed together, the emphasis of these workshops was on exploration: of opening and writing new perspectives, of a refusal to be confined by expectations, language or form. Poets were encouraged to write and perform authentically, and we have endeavoured to retain their poetic voices by presenting their work as close to its original, performed form as possible.

The poems included in this anthology demonstrate the wide popular appeal of poetry, as well as its therapeutic value. In the near future, we will take this project to other locations in South Africa and, hopefully, beyond to further explore the transformative power of poetry.

This anthology contains poems that are meant to be performed and not merely read. Performances from the two workshops, many of which relate to poems within this collection, can be seen at www.poetrynonscenes.com and www.zapp.org.za.

We would like to thank the External Engagement Committee of the Department of History at University College London, who kindly funded this publication, as well as uHlanga for their interest in the collection.

Part I
Conflict

Mirrors
Shade K. Olugbosi

As my mother spoke
Her comforting lies concealed my tiny ears
From the echoes of the screams escaping from
    the gas chambers

Her maternal breath cleansed the air
Of the
stench
of burnt corpses
By cradling me in a veil of a vain child's dreams

My mother told me once
That under their striped pyjamas
Each face is a mirror
Of one's soul
My teary eyes couldn't see it then
As I stared down the streets of the ghetto:
Shards of broken glass polluted the ground in
    heavy piles of dejection

My mother
Hunched over
Searched for the remnants of my baby brother

I can see it clearly now
His hollow cheeks streaked with pale salty lines
His frail body a product of Germany's crimes

I understand now
That if one's face were a mirror, a reflection of
 one's soul
His mutilated face was desolate
Because his life was no more

The Only Thing Left
After Kopano Maroga's "it's been so long"
Dshamilja Roshani

Where do we begin?
Where do we begin?
Let us begin in the present
for it is the only thing we all share.

I.
The country I was born in
(yet often struggle to call home)
has now been silent for six months.
How do we speak about a thing
that is not allowed a name?
Apparently we cannot call it genocide,
apparently we cannot call it Apartheid,
apparently these words are too burdened with history
to be dragged into the present.
I wonder whose history was burdened with them,
whose present is undeserving of them,
whose futures are being murdered.
I wonder whose words hold the power
to end a thing without a name.

II.
At the family dinner,
my mother dishes up her steaming tahdig,
this remnant of our blended heritage
crunching golden between our teeth.
It is hard to speak while our mouths are full
but I am fed up with the silence.
"Amma, what did our family do during the Holocaust?"
My grandmother,
this woman with a heart-shaped face,
wipes her mouth before she speaks.
"My father helped our Jewish neighbours to hide,"
she says and folds her napkin – stainless, white.
I remember a study I read
which found that about 30 percent of Germans today
believe their family to have helped Jewish people
   during Hitler's regime –
in reality it was 0.3 percent.
Memory can be a convenient beast.
I want to believe Amma,
but history's statistics pile up between us
and I digest the broken silence.

> > >

III.
My grandfather is not here anymore
to complain about his daughter's food.
His country is the one
Hitler stole the word Aryan from:
a self-designation of Iranic people
misconstrued into a German superior race.
How strange,
when none of his children and children's children
are considered Aryan today,
neither here nor there.

IV.
My grandfather's country
(the one that robbed him of a home)
claims to support Palestine.
The same country whose regime
me and my Iranian, Kurdish and Palestinian friends
fought against last year.
Jin, Jiyan, Azadî!
Marg bar dictator!
Woman, Life, Freedom!
Down with the dictator!
we screamed, casting echoes
of a distant revolution onto Berlin's streets.
But Karl Marx had already warned us
that all things are pregnant with their contrary.
So here we are, once again
watching monsters being born everywhere,
tossed namelessly into our laps.

I wonder if I will still fight back
once I have reached Amma's age,
or if I will cradle a beast of my own memory.
I wonder if I too will have grandchildren
who will refuse to feast in silence
and ask me what I did back then
during the thing without a name.

V.
Amma remembers the spring of 1967
when Iran's last Shah had come to visit Berlin.
*"We were all there, protesting,
your three-year-old mother on my shoulders."*
The regime was different but the reasons the same,
the Shah did fall but the monsters remained.

VI.
Amma says she does not care
what name we give the thing
currently happening in Gaza.
"It is horrible and it must end."
If only her country would listen to her
instead of dropping death from distant skies
while police beat up those who dare to speak up
and deport Brown bodies who disagree.
If only her country was a history student
that learned a principle instead of a rule.

> > >

VII.
I am learning
that history birthed far too many nameless monsters
tossed into far too many nameless laps
saddled into far too many nameless backs
dragged into far too many nameless directions
consuming far too many nameless futures
to be squeezed into a linear timeline

Where do we begin?
Where do we begin?
Let us begin in the present
for it is the only thing we have left
to change.

Time Echoes of Sorrow
Amanda Majola

In shadows cast by darkest days
Echoes haunt where silence lays
Screams unheard, lost in the fray
Memories stained, they cannot sway.

Fields once green, now soaked in red
Where innocence and hope have fled
A tearful plea, a whispered prayer
But anguish hangs heavy in the air.

Generations lost, their stories untold
In hearts and minds, their horror holds.
Yet amidst the pain, a flicker of light
Resilience blooms, refusing the night.

With solemn words we pledge anew
To honour those we never knew
For, in our hearts, their spirits reside
Forever remembered, never denied.

Genocide
Elizabeth Makanha-Dhliwayo

The taunting sounds of gunshots, bombs …
The deafening sounds
Of men, women and children
Joined the musical beat in wailing
As they are lead like a sheep to be slaughtered

The smell of hatred, rage and anger
Suffocates and ravages my innocence
Leaving me clothed in the devil's tunic
Coveting vengeance … but how?

Time is a silly friend, it waits for no man
It's either I seek revenge, or escape for dear life
For genocide knows no division nor subtraction
But only multiplication and addition
I see them, hundreds, thousands, millions … slain
No names attached to their bodies anymore
Do some people count less than others?
Before I become a number, let me …
The hungry graves make me infuriated
With their eternal appetite
For they gulped them ruthlessly
Leaving bloody clothes, shoes, utensils …
As symbols of unsaid goodbyes
Anyway, as I drown in anger, depressed,
I will just say
"G-o-o-d b-y-e to you all … since names matter no more."

The Water in Gaza
Kiara Braum

In any case there is nothing
beyond
where you come from
No place to go
when you know
your own sky.
I can't write about anything like
terror
The great disservice of language
non posso
ek kan nie
You sit on your heels and dream of your ancestors,
where they welcome each other and
nobody cries.
They speak about you like you can write about war
like war doesn't happen
like you only write poems because you
know
no war
You know, no war ever happens without the great
  service of language
The river and the sea speak the same dialect
Some do not know this,
between the river and the sea
is the bridge
of great understanding and
war; understanding; burnt down

> > >

In Fishhoek the blaze
almost took
the house
where my cousins live and pray and hope and eat
In Gaza, it did.
It takes.
In Gaza people are praying before they wake up
   before they can breathe before they can
The ancestors: too close now
to see ahead
Ancestors clinging onto heels,
this one is mine
this one is mine
this one is mine
this one, don't forget us.
Don't
remember the sound of a language before
you remember your family.
Forget the blaze when you come.
Think of the water and its lexicon,
think of the way that it rushes to God
think of how it joins its brother,
and is lost in its kin
think of rejoining and becoming
something big
God will not forget this.
Do you understand what it means to speak freely?
What it means to cross a bridge that is not
   occupied or weakened?
You understand that water also drowns if provoked
by earthquakes.
The earth quakes now,
Language too.

Maja
Denise Newfield

How old were you, Maja,
beautiful ballerina,
with a turned out leg and
a perfectly pointed toe?

How old when the men called you and
you packed your ballet shoes
into a suitcase?
Your familiar life
disappeared in a puff
that puff turned into
the deathsmoke of your parents

How did you survive?
Was it ballet dreams,
pirouettes in the darkness
in your salmon pink slippers
while a mountain of shoes
tied together in pairs
grew
outside the gas chambers –
contribution to the war effort.

> > >

Later
was it liberation
relief
guilt, joy or grief
for those lost
while you, a teen now, were found?

Where did you go then –
barefoot, sans ballet shoes
the long cold 'death march'
to a place unknown?

How did you retain that beauty
for sixty years
your ballerina figure
your upright stance?

Is that why you were quiet
hardly spoke
hair coiffed but
a blank face
and only a faint smile?

Your picture on the wall
in the Before Hall …
Is that why he designed
this museum for you?

Part II
Bodies and Emotions

Children in their Twenties
Rachel Freeme

My mind is a merry-go-round of ever-
   changing thoughts.
I get dizzy with them, sick with them
I'm out of my mind and everybody knows it.
But as long as you humour me, I'll have an
   outlet for angry poetry
Because pain is art, but sometimes
I'm jealous of your immaturity despite the
   consequences.
Reckless freedom breeds alcoholism but at
   least you're having fun.
Gas station condoms are cheaper, you tell me,
   and your friend's mom buys you weed.
Become your favourite rock star and try to
   believe the lyrics you write, that
Life is too long to live
Kill yourself slowly
With boredom and cigarettes.
Anything worth doing has already been done.

Languishing on my Bed
Katlego Malema

Mentally exhausted
and bone-weary,
like an ear from an overplayed tune.

I spend all day
lamenting the death of my ardour.
With discontinued motivation,
my psyche comes apart at the seams.

On my tod
as the lonely sea at night.
Devoid of the desire
to bestir myself.
The body lays helplessly,
whilst the void continues to augment.

At its best, this is languishment.

Wall Street
Ivai Nyamutsamba

I live in a time
Lost forever
Poke the apeman's eye
He'll pull the lever
Its tales live forever
Like diamonds are forever
A meisie's best friend
Fake smiles like Mona Lisa
Trades smiles for frowns
Like diamonds on Wall Street
From tears of joy
To tears of pain
Keep an eye on the healer
Follow his steps
To see the Sandman at work
Listen to the youth
They the culture
Listen to the you the youth
They the future
Cocoa brown babes
Busy bees
Bundle your nectar
Night shall creep in like a thief in the night
So the vulture
Roam high and low
Fly high and low
The tides of the Styx roar like Galilee at night
Walk on water like Peter

Only the night knows what Peter saw
Only the night knows
The heart of the night vulture

The Collector
Sharon Rose

I am not in love with you,
I am just a poet.
And you are
Just another butterfly
With more things to add to my collection.
My collection of pretty things
My collection of delicate things
My collection of soon-to-be-dead things with a place in
   my graveyard.
Don't let the flowers in my hands
The flowers in my hair
The flowers on my tongue fool you.
They are not real flowers
But there is a tombstone with your name on it.
I may not know how to grow flowers
But I do know how to dig.
I only know how to dig
And bury
And make you think this is a garden.
That is why you came, isn't it?
For the flowers
And not the coffin
Not this second cocoon
You came for a chance at rebirth
To get stronger, better wings, isn't it?
How can I possibly gift you something I have never had?

I only have the gift of illusion
And that I have unveiled in abundance.
A coffin made up of flowers is still a coffin
And you are
Its rightful owner.
You are
Just another muse I will strip bare of beauty and grace.
I hope you understand.
I am just an admirer.
An honest collector.
Of only the prettiest wings.

October 23
Tshegofatso Masemola

Isn't it funny how everything comes to an end?

From strangers to lovers.
Then lovers to strangers again.

All the promises we made vanished into thin air.
They say promises are made to be broken.

But not in this way.

I didn't expect you to be perfect.
But that didn't mean you should've been disloyal.
You knew how much I loved you.
And you still did it.
"What did I do?"

You slept with a stranger in our bed.
You allowed them to get your attention.

Should I forgive you?
For my sanity, I will forgive you.

But I will never forget October 23rd.

The God of Bonsai
Nicole Best

The God of Bonsai
is not a wizened stranger,
winter-skinned-apple-face, a kindly crinkle.

He comes to me on a Saturday night
as I hang laundry in the air of ice and smoke.
He is unpractised in the give-and-take
of first conversation.
I think him rude.

He will leave the country soon.
He will take with him
his wife, his children, his lack of social grace.

He will not take the bonsai;
the shrunken trees he has not watered in months;
the bare branches his own skeleton.

He will not take the bonsai;
he will plant them somewhere in good soil,
a bare corner of red-fleshed land.

He will not take the bonsai;
they will be ready when he calls them,
numb to cold, and drought, and lack.

He will not take the bonsai.

They will not need him.

Border Gate
Katlego Choshi

Stand for hours at a border gate
Checking passports
Am I a pawn in this game of hate

You shall not pass
Turn back or else
Friend or foe
No you shall not go

What's your purpose in this country
Did you come here chasing money
Or did you come to bring more hatred and trafficking

Once I put my finger on this trigger
Your chances of passing by me get slimmer
If we find you in my country
Siyak'dudula
We see you down the street
Siyak'dubula

Depression
Delyne Nyasha Madziva

Hello depression, we meet again
You were part of my teenage life
Like a demo, stuck beside me.
Do you remember how you would
Make me go to sleep crying?
Painting my walls black
Making my mother thinking, I got an attitude.

A killer in a head
A rainbow turns black
A silver lining goes into hiding
And into thin air, my emotions vanish
I have emotional bruises to show.

Everything I touch cracks
My heart lost its spark
It now gossips with my pains
Because I have now failed.

You brought me flames
And you put me through hell
But like a rock,
I survived and I'm still standing.

> > >

My vision became blurred
My confidence reduced into self-disgust
A smile hides my internal wounds
Suicide answers every question in my head
I ponder about it, yet it's not the answer.

Hello and bye
Depression

My old friend

This is a Poem
Kekana Phologo

Empty vessel, of elegant screams

Plucked into the ground
Shed light to the grass
Temporarily they are one

One bites, whilst one swallows
Roots uprooted, reflection by still
Self-introspection, confused realisation

Memory by heart, emotionless at source
Self is the course (cause), a descending journey
Filled with turmeric, yet so bitter

A three-wayed net of locks
A transparent bucket, of colourless potions
A wooden mechanic, rusting at heart

Endless journeys, of unlimited limits
Bright shadows, weared by truthful liars
A uniform of colours, painting upon one another

An empty vessel, of elegant screams

Baby
Busisiwe Kgosi

Oh how I've missed you my love
there is such a calm commotion that comes
   with you
A groove that puts my soul in check
You are a fine dining experience for myself,
   with only me in the restaurant, I'd hope
There is a calm and an ocean that comes
   with the way you stare at me
I know it's not love, I know it's just reminiscing
You calm my racing heart, you cultivate a
   gentleness I had since forgotten in childhood
   out of me
Looking at you is like looking at myself
I want to be kind to you
Running my eyes over what you look like now,
   your face, your gaze, your lips, your cheeks
It is like running my calloused hands down the
   most peaceful part of my life, and
I'm blind
Oh how I miss you my love, you never cease to
   provoke a calmness in me
I want to protect this heart of mine that
   exists in you, you are the most beautiful thing
   about the war that lived in me
That lives in me
You bring me peace

Ink
Sabrina Alho

My body was once blank:
A clean and crisp sheet of paper.
But now, it's stained with ink,
the seams tearing as ink bleeds through.
Thin pieces of tape hold it together.
Soon they will rip and be carried away by the wind.
I am utterly ruined.

No longer does my body belong to me alone.
My body belongs to their gazes and hands.
Their gazes were once harmless,
light pencil marks that could be erased
with the flick of a wrist.

Their hands were once harmless as well,
hidden within their pockets.
Everything felt harmless
until their hands stained my skin
with their ink-covered fingertips.

Now their gaze feels like a dark pencil mark
that will erase but still mark my skin.

I wish to tear off the tape before the wind can,
so that maybe
I can further ruin myself.
If I am ruined enough,
no one else will want to mark me with their ink.

Part III
Gender and Identity

Dear Black Boys
Ntokozo Twala

Black boys don't acknowledge the sun anymore
    like they used to
even though their skin is brown, tinged with gold
as the sun, our one and only true lover
does not hesitate to let it glow

Black girls' hazel eyes have hardened due to
    constant rejection from those they
birth but yet are here to mourn.
It seems as though for our sons that
being black is a death sentence
and they're buried before they're born

See we're gathered here today
to lay those stolen from their mother's womb,
    those whose umbilical cord was
ripped off
and were fed the fruit of hatred
Hatred for the skin they possess and their
    mothers, because we look like them
So, we pray, we pray the sun never sets on you
Like it did on us

Because as black women we were exposed to
    gunshots in the form of
degradation fired by white men but given
    instructions by black men desperately

begging for them to pull the trigger as if they
    wouldn't turn the guns on them
once we were dead

But even in my last moments, I am expected to
    love my fallen soldier
For it is not his fault that the world has forsaken
    him and even though I too have
been mutilated by the swords of racism and your
    daggers of hate
I will treat your wounds because my love for you is
    stronger than the hatred you
Spew

I can't say I'm I when I'm considered "ghetto" in
    the eyes of a black man
Lesser in those of a white man
But yet you'll always see me as a sexual object,
    so I'm always told to look out
I'm sorry but unlike black men I couldn't afford to
    sell out
See you wouldn't be able to tell with how foul
    those mouths are, that they've
been breastfed by those darkened nipples
I'm sorry does that make you feel uncomfortable?
More uncomfortable than the desensitisation of
    a black woman's pain?

> > >

And her stifled screams
More uncomfortable than the bullets that seep
   into his skin?
That I will have to dig out
Cause who else will do it?
The white women you glamourise at the expense
   of these hardened eyes

Oh no wait, the black girls that fit the standard
   cause at least they're
westernised
See I don't know what hurts the most, the fact
   that we'll never stop loving you or
that you'll always see your dark skin as a curse

Making Tea
Ilanit Furman

Today I will make you tea
As you have asked
With your eyes still red
And your body still squashed

And I hope the warmth of the liquid
Will run over the sad history
Of your life
And soothe it
Like healing waters

For you are a woman
Who must live with regret
And the dream of a different life
And a different man
And a choice that was wrong
And cannot be unchosen

What a heavy sadness
To carry around

Let me make you your tea
As you have asked
It is the least I can do

The Epic Quest for Socks
Tania Nobantu Ngindana

There once was a sock, oh so grand,
Lost its mate in a foreign land,
It hopped and it skipped, and it rolled about,
Searching for its partner tout.

Through the drawers and 'neath the bed,
It looked for the one it thought had fled,
In the laundry pile, it took a dive,
Emerging with a single sock to survive.

Oh, the adventures this sock did face,
In a world where socks had lost their place,
It faced off with a fuzzy dusty bunny,
And it tripped over a rubber ducky funny.

But lo and behold, under the chair,
Was its mate, the missing pair!
Together at last, they danced with glee,
A silly sock reunion for all to see.

And so the tale of the socks was told,
Hilarious and wacky, silly and bold,
For in the world of feet and toes,
Even socks can have epic woes.

Armed with a Smile
Jolene Raison

"Smile!
You're prettier when you smile,"
said the man
like so many other men
like too many other men.
And so I did and maybe I was
and all he saw in my smile
       – I'm sure –
was the promise of
a trinket to be palmed,
a flower to be plucked,
a sugar candy to be sucked,
like so many men
like too many men,
not
the blade that is sheathed,
the bomb that is unarmed,
the gun that is holstered.

"Come, smile for me!"
Smile? For you?
Oh, I will come
and I will smile!
I will come for you with my smile,
me
and other women
      so many women
           more and more women.

                    > > >

We will come for you with our smiles,
with our pretty smiles,
but know:
when we come for you
it will be
with smiles that are unsheathed,
with smiles that are armed and ticking,
with smiles that are locked and loaded.

African
Sandisiwe Dlamini

Ngingum'Africa
Ngigqize ngevatha ngob'Africa
Ngingum'Africa
Ngihlabahlosile ngoju lobuhle
Nobuhlakani bekhethelo

Ngifana nesiziba esicwebile, sacweba ukuzedlula zonke
Ngingumphumela wephupho, elaphushwa ilabo
Abafika kuqala kunami,
Ezimpandeni zami
Nginjenjembali ehlume edwaleni
Yaqede yathela izithelo zobuhle nobuhlakani
Ngiyala ukwehluleka lapho sebengehlulela
Kakade ngigqize ngevatha ngob'Africa
Ngiyazigqaja ngobumina.

How is My Hair?
Olive Olusegun

how is my hair oppression and resurrection?
augmented perceptions
revolutions
involuntary constitutions
wild contusions
of fingers tangling abstractly into braids
ends burnt like sage
my hair is a bird and a cage
freedom or a cave
something wild
or something to be tamed
makes white masses enraged
and black men still enslaved
to the idea of white women as wonder
so my hair must
be suppressed under
drowned beneath waves of weaves
so she submerges herself every month to
   maintain her white identity

alternatively ...
burning boisterous black afro ends of black
   babies has become a ritual
because bantu knots are seen as too political
so you relax her
under relaxers
because straight hair imitates

Cleopatra
Mona Lisa
the golden ratio

now she is worthy of a beauty standard never made for shades of indigo

so in she goes
to the salon every month
to commit suicide
killing crevices of her identity for which her ancestors died
but now with every stride
she gets compliments
a clean
contained
cosmopolitan
black woman
who is no longer a threat

because before, oh the clients were worried right
"what does her bald head mean?"
"her black panther afro screams she automatically likes to hang white people by the noose!"
before the aunties and the mothers were worried right

> > >

"her dreadlocks are too long ... "
"she is trying to seduce husbands into
   temptation."
"her untamed mountain of mane means she
   must not be serious about her life!"
"did you see her braids are colourful?
   ooooh, that one! she must go out all night."

when will the black woman's hair not be a
   decodable diabolical dictionary?
a political dictionary
a condemnation calligraphy
a hieroglyphery upon which we must hanged
when will a black woman's hair
not be augmented and enslaved to each
   and everyone's demands

so for once and for all
we pray
RELEASE YOUR HANDS!

… Flashes!
Mpho Mametja

I still remember!
I remember his eyes pregnant with pride,
When he gazed at me like an animal that has its eye set on a prey … For in his eyes, I wasn't human, I wasn't woman, I wasn't just a child! And whether I was just 18, 16, 12 or even 9 years of age,
He didn't bother to ask.
To him I was just a thing born to feed his masculine needs,
And come rain or hail he will get me to submit,
Even if it meant inflicting a lifetime worth of pain in just 18 minutes.
He whispered to me "Gothwe mosadi o swara thipa ka bogaleng."

See, he lost me there cause I am certain that I am still years away from being addressed as "mosadi".
His voice, it, it still echoes in my mind every now and then.
The scars he left engraved on my body like fine art.
When he clutched his claws into my skin,
They will forever serve as a painful reminder.

See, I used to walk along these streets full of trust in humanity.
"Lefase le eme ka maoto." I've heard that before.
It's just always been too far from home.
But he! He dared to look me in my eyes,
He found pleasure in my vulnerability

> > >

He dared to touch my hands, suck them of their retaliating power.
With his cold, cold blood-filled hands,
He dared to silence me.
He addressed himself "monnatia",
Said my cries were like sweet melodies to his ears,
That me laying there powerless, floating in the pool of blood,
With my face smeared with tears
My body shivering in pain
Somehow comfirmed his "manhood".
He addressed me as "Sweetheart".
He had his way with me
He satisfied himself
With my honour! My innocence!
He dared to infiltrate my garden,
Pluck out all its flowers.
He dared to leave me empty.
He, he planted the first seed of hatred.

And they! The ones that vowed to serve me justice
Maybe my dressing, or the way I moved, the way I looked at him,
Maybe my "No" wasn't strong or too convincing.
Maybe when he waved at me, I should have kept my teeth hidden behind lips because for some reason that miraculously translates into a yes in the more realistic world they said
They said I should be more careful next time
I watched as they jotted down my name next to the word "victim"
And that fiddled with my whole existence.

But I, the girl in front of you today
God says she's not a victim, she is a conqueror.
She is not responsible for his tainted soul
For his long dead conscience.
She is more than just part of statistics.
She is human, she is woman and she is a child
And enough is enough!

Springbok
Imange Lobese

Easy prey for the predators,
Yet you devour them with grace.
You leap into the future with boundless energy
But slow down to observe
and take a drink from the river of gold where
   your heart is pure.

Your heart unites a nation,
the Rainbow Nation of springboks,
each on a different path to survival.
But leaping into the future,
together you thrive.

With every bound,
you leave the past behind,
And forge a new trail,
where freedom is your guide.
Your spirit is unbreakable.
You are unshakeable.
You are the symbol of hope,
for a brighter tomorrow.

I Miss the Dolls And Toys
Choaro Letsoha

Dear inner child
I know that you've been haunted, wounded and taunted
by the vivid memories
you like to think you have left behind
I feel like it's been centuries
from our last encounter
maybe it's for the best
to avoid unwanted banter
between you and I
to enter my heart
and tour the disgustingly filthy rooms
known as horrific trauma
as I'd like them to just be tombs
I know while you're reading this you're crying
so I'm sorry
knowing very well that you deserve closure
which is a risk that I'm not willing to take
as I will be an emotional wreck
this the stinging truth as I didn't want to be fake
well, I guess we need healing
so why not take the risk
and let's start our journey today
as I'm quite unprepared
but I think
I need to pay you a visit
once again my old friend.

The Portrait of a South Asian Woman
Diyoni Harisinghe

In visions cast by biased gaze,
a South Asian woman stands.
Her worth determined by the paleness of her skin,
the curves she possesses,
the spikes of black hair adorning her skin,
where prejudice still commands.

Her coffee skin, a canvas rich and deep,
painted by histories untold.
Yet, in the eyes of those who sleep,
she is nothing but a mere damsel.
She is nothing but a servant.
She is nothing but a wife.

They weave a web of lies,
inscribed with ignorance.
Stereotypes written by kings;
poison given by kings;
cruelty painted by kings,
dignity not in their hearts.

But in her spirit, fierce and true,
resides a strength untamed.
With roots that stretch amidst her bloodline,
a tenacious trait drilled in her essence,
wearing the cloak of culture's embrace on her saree,
her spirit remains unyielding,
her soul remains divine.

The Burnt Pot
Leya Muthen

I'm a pot on a stove
I stand alone, aflame
filled to the brim
boiling, bubbling, brewing.
I overflow
little by little.
My promise of nurture and substance dissipates
until there's nothing left but cremated remains
   that gain a red glow
and rancid smell.
I crackle, I hiss, I sputter.
I stand empty and alone
Burning, busted, broke.

I Am
Laeeqa Ebrahim

I wish I was good at poetry.
But I am not.
I am a writer, yes.
Twisting and fabricating stories is my passion,
My talent.
The thing I consider myself good at.
But I am not a poet.

Perhaps if I was more creative.
Or read it aloud with the confidence of a boring,
   pretentious middle-aged man.
Maybe then I would be a poet.
But I am not.

What is worse is this:
I am not the poem either.
A clichéd ideal I am aware.

But
There is no elaborate, spontaneous, earth-
   shattering admiration being thrown at me.
No desperate, desirable longing for me.

Yes, there is the usual "angsty, teenage" void
Hidden somewhere that I choose to ignore –
My own longing for something.
What? I cannot decipher.

Love?
Recognition?
Understanding?
Bonding?
Acknowledgement?

I don't know.
But there is something there.

Yes, I am not a poet and
I am not the poem.

I don't know what I am or who I am or where I
   am or why I am or how I am or even when I am.
But words are fun and often feelings can be too
Even when I am unsure of what the feelings are
   exactly
The important part is that I feel them.

The weird itchy swirling pit in my chest
At 3 a.m. on a Friday morning when I can't sleep
   that leads me to write my first real, raw,
   unfiltered piece of work.
The deep rich sticky delight at roughly 4 p.m.
When the sun hits the brownstone of the
   neighbours' house just right and I feel like a
   child in a dream.

                                                             > > >

The painful tension behind the eyes when a
    song I last heard 6 years ago
Plays randomly in a mall or on a car radio
And I sit there and think
Damn.

Perhaps, I am not a poet or a poem or an
    adequate author or a good daughter
    or a kind friend or a valued learner or an
    interesting character or a pined-after love

But

I am something. And I feel many somethings.
In my heart and my chest and my bones and
    my blood and my eyes and my mouth and my
    stomach and my skin and my head and my
    brain and my fingers.

I am something.
I am someone.
I am somewhere.
I am some reason.
I am some time.

And I write.

I could be a poet.
And I could be a poem.

Perhaps
Not someone else's, but I could be.
And perhaps I want to be.
And perhaps I can be.
And perhaps
I am.

About the editors

Tom Penfold is a researcher of contemporary South African poetry and performance culture. His 2017 monograph *Black Consciousness and South Africa's National Literature* explored how Black Consciousness poets shaped the direction of South African politics. His *History of Post-Apartheid South Africa* will be published by Routledge in 2026. Tom has held teaching positions at University College London and the University of Birmingham. and is a Research Associate at the University of Johannesburg and the University of the Witwatersrand.

Adam Levin is a researcher in the Department of English at the University of the Witwatersand, and a senior member of the South African Poetry Project (ZAPP). His research focuses on how the academic field of memory studies can be utilised in studies of community engagement, education, and poetry. His work has been featured in *Holocaust Studies*, *English Studies in Africa*, *Literature, Critique and Empire Today*, and *Safundi*. Adam also serves as the Vice-Executive Secretary on the executive board of the International Network of Genocide Scholars (INoGS), and as a Research Associate of the African Centre for the Study of the United States (ACSUS).

Deirdre Byrne is a Professor of English at the University of South Africa, and the Director of ZAPP (the South African Poetry Project). Her research focuses on the representation of gender in literary texts, especially in speculative fiction and in women's poetry. Her work has been published in *Foundation* and *Extrapolation* as well as in *Education as Change*. She has recently completed a co-authored book on the poetry of Jane Hirshfield. She has been writing poetry since she was a child.

POETRYNONSCENES.COM
ZAPP.ORG.ZA
UHLANGAPRESS.CO.ZA